I0821031

SHIPS AHOY!
Fishing Vessels
by Kaitlyn Duling
BLASTOFF! 2 READERS
BLASTOFF! READERS, AN IMPRINT OF BELLWETHER MEDIA BY FLUTTERBEE

Blastoff! Readers are carefully developed by literacy experts to build reading stamina and move students toward fluency by combining standards-based content with developmentally appropriate text.

LEVELS

Level 1 provides the most support through repetition of high-frequency words, light text, predictable sentence patterns, and strong visual support.

Level 2 offers early readers a bit more challenge through varied sentences, increased text load, and text-supportive special features.

Level 3 advances early-fluent readers toward fluency through increased text load, less reliance on photos, advancing concepts, longer sentences, and more complex special features.

★ **Blastoff! Universe**

Reading Level

Grade K

Grades 1–3

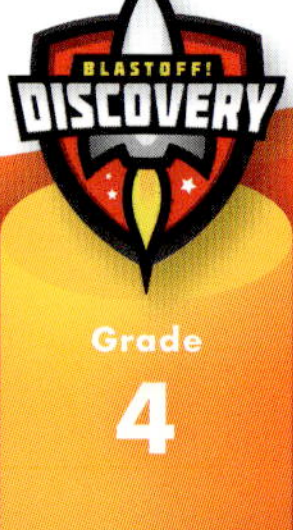

Grade 4

This edition first published in 2026 by Bellwether Media, Inc.

For information regarding permission, write to Bellwether Media, Inc., Attention: Permissions Department, 3500 American Blvd W, Suite 150, Bloomington, MN 55431.

Library of Congress Cataloging-in-Publication Data is available at www.loc.gov or upon request from the publisher.

ISBN: 9798893048001 (hardcover)
ISBN: 9798893049008 (ebook)

Editor: Kieran Downs Designer: Jennifer Bowyer

Printed in the United States of America, North Mankato, MN.

Table of Contents

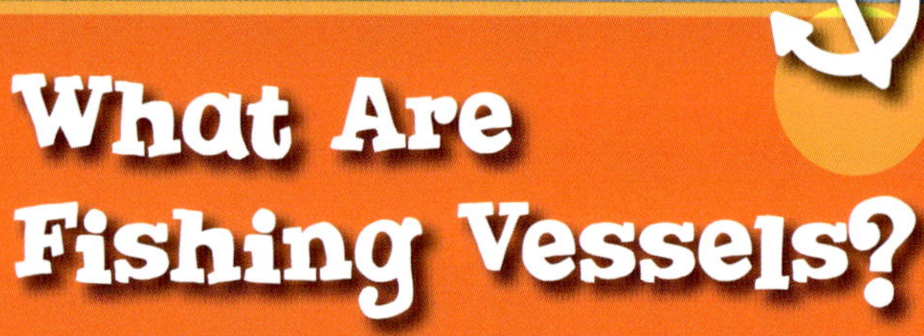

What Are Fishing Vessels?

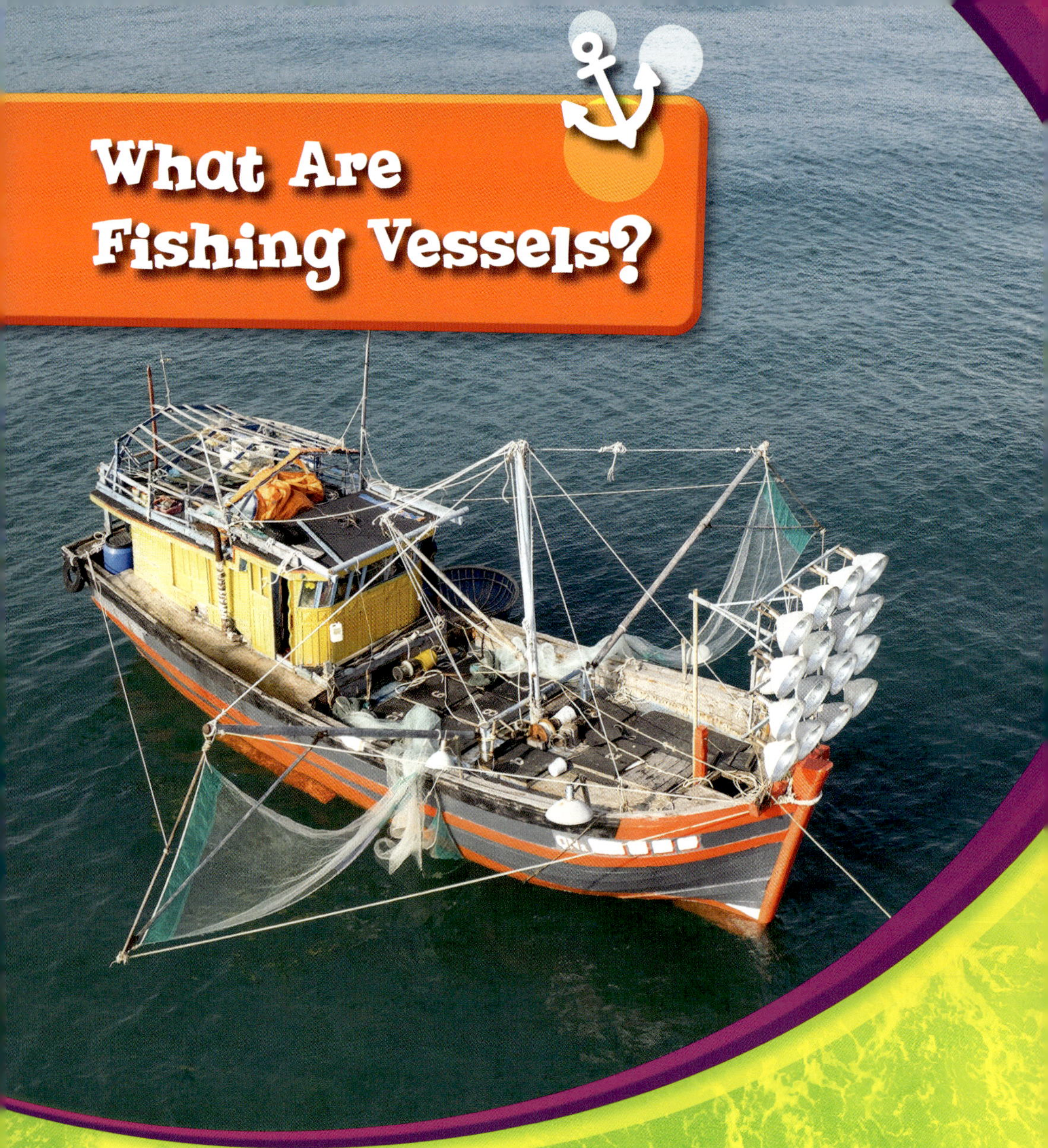

Fishing vessels are ships used to catch fish and other sea life.

They travel on seas, lakes, and rivers.

Fishing vessels carry nets and other tools to catch fish.

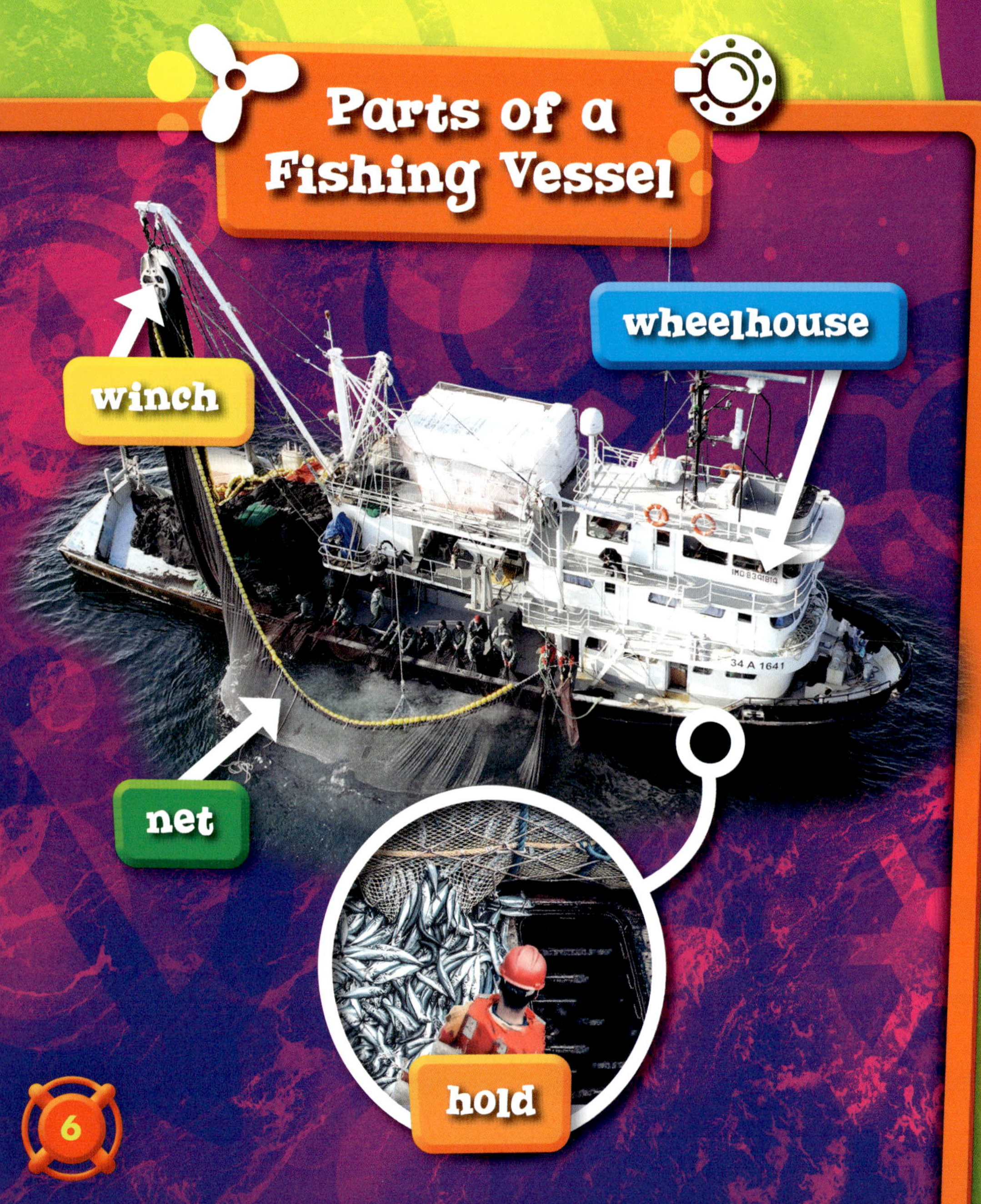

A **winch** is used to move heavy nets on and off the ship.

Fish are stored in **holds**. Cold fish holds keep the fish fresh.

Fishing vessels are controlled in the wheelhouse.

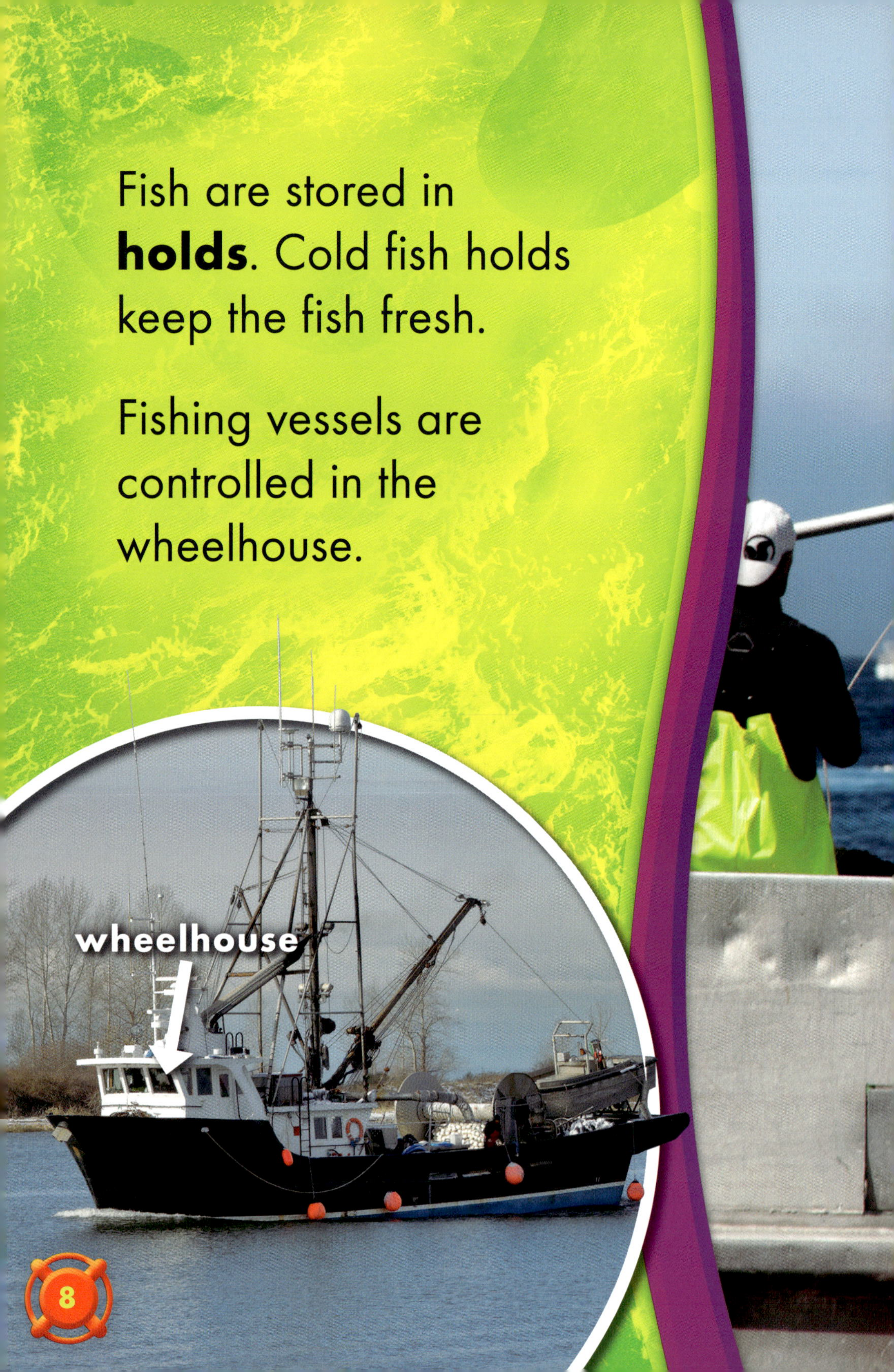

hold

Types of Fishing Vessels

trawler

seiner

line vessel

trap setter

Trawlers drag underwater nets. **Seiners** use nets that close around fish.

Line vessels drag **fishing lines** with **bait** and hooks. Trap setters catch **shellfish**.

What a Catch!

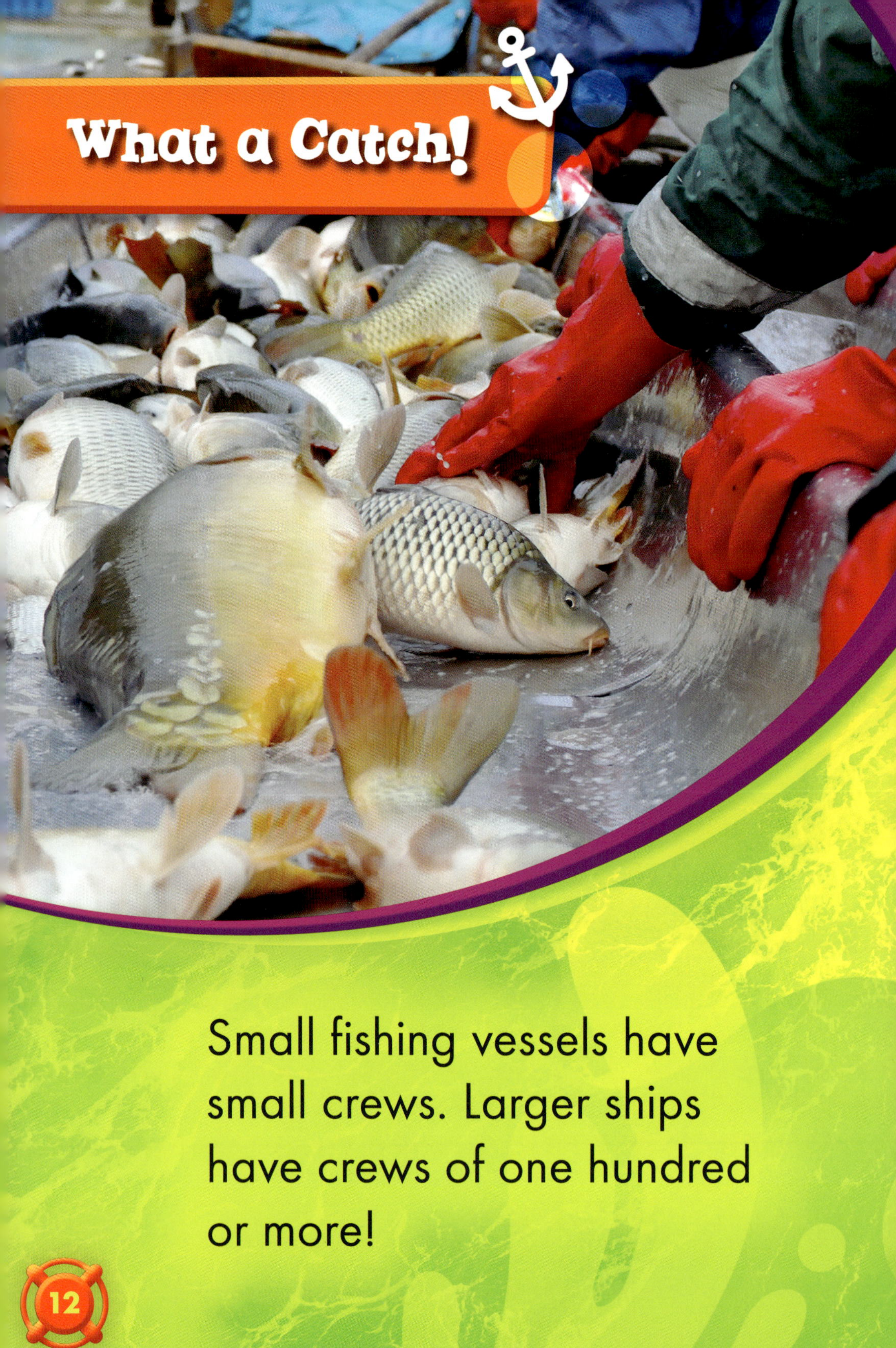

Small fishing vessels have small crews. Larger ships have crews of one hundred or more!

The biggest ships have space to clean, cut, and freeze fish.

Ship Stats

Lunar Bow

Size 262.5 feet (80 meters) long; 52.5 feet (16 meters) wide

Type trawler

Top Speed 17.5 knots (20 miles or 32 kilometers per hour)

Purpose catching different kinds of fish

The captain steers the ship from the wheelhouse.

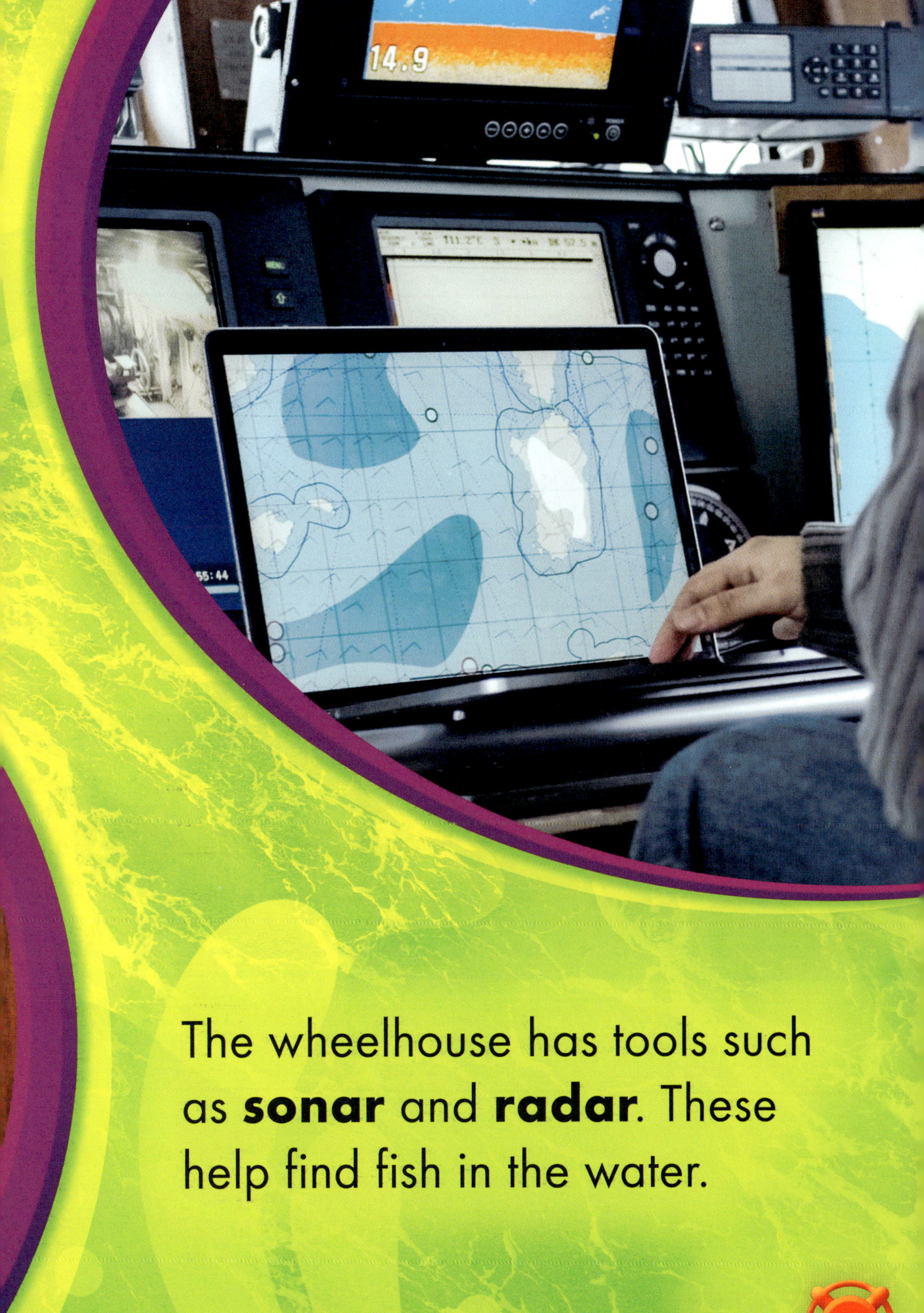

The wheelhouse has tools such as **sonar** and **radar**. These help find fish in the water.

Deckhands catch and store fish. They use nets, lines, or traps.

Purse Seining

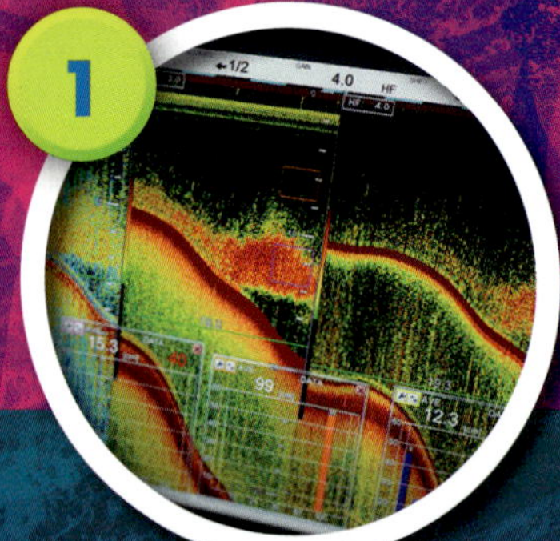

Tools are used to find a large group of fish.

The boat moves the purse seine net around the fish. The top of the net floats and the bottom sinks.

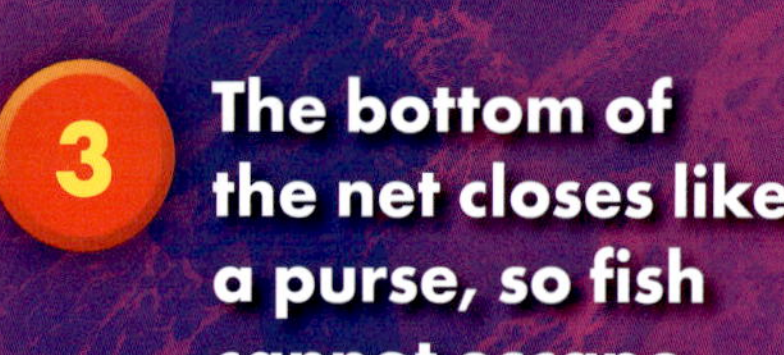

The bottom of the net closes like a purse, so fish cannot escape.

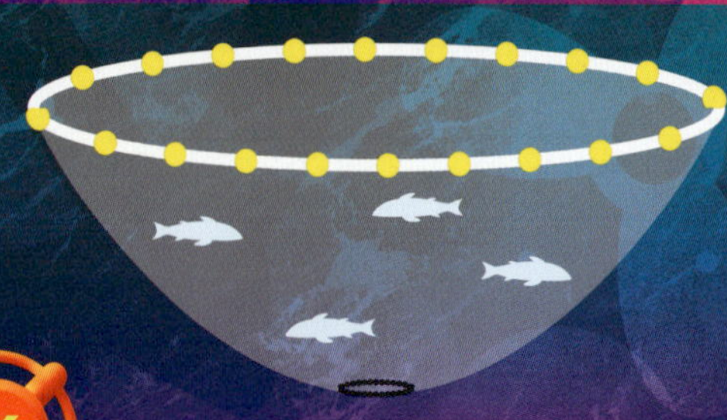

The net is brought onto the fishing vessel.

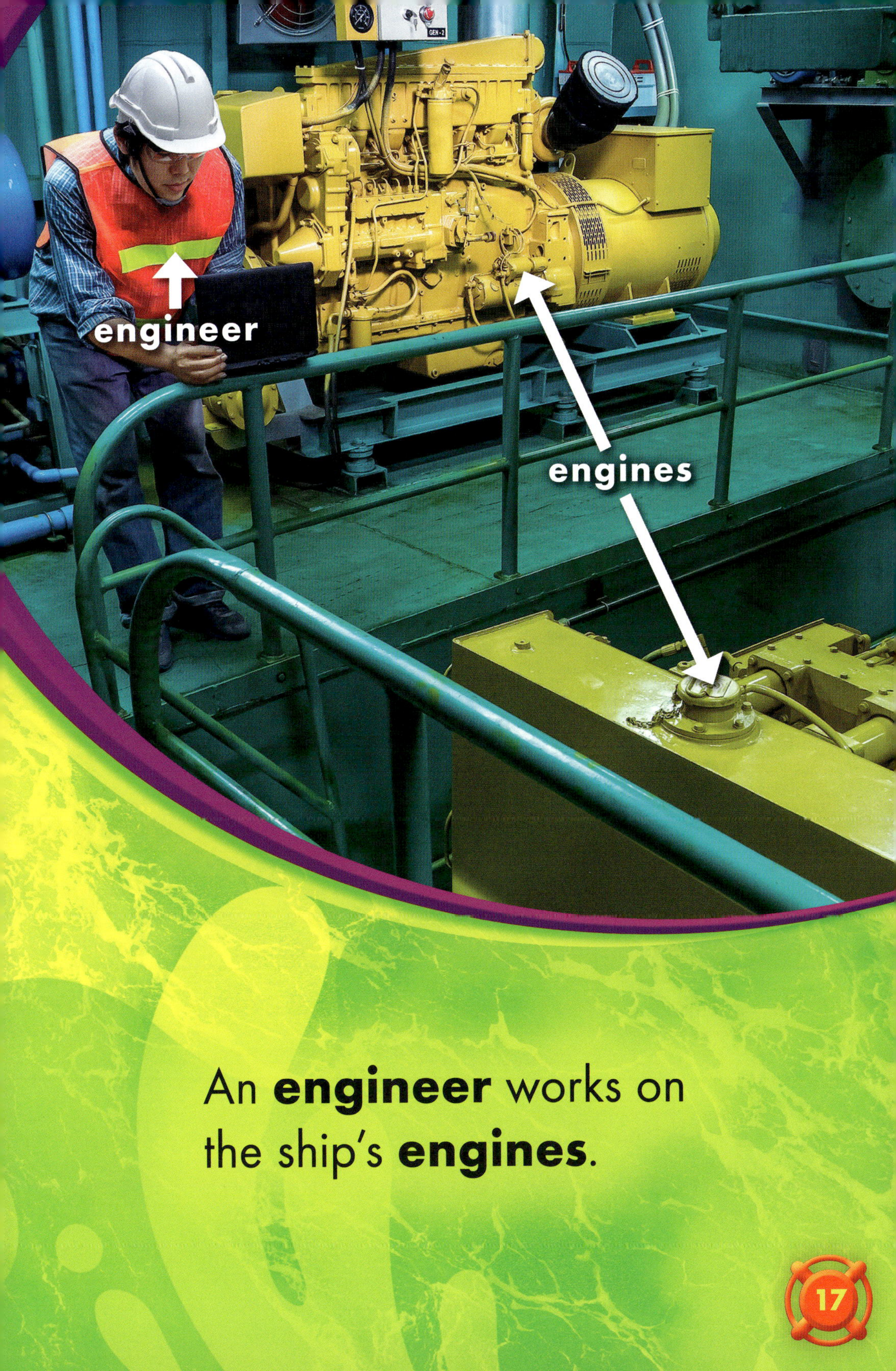

An **engineer** works on the ship's **engines**.

Fishing vessels have strong engines. Most can travel around 9.5 **knots** (11 miles or 17.7 kilometers per hour).

Slower speeds help the nets and lines move through the water.

Feeding the World

People all over the world eat food caught by fishing vessels.

Fishing vessels help us get fish, shrimp, and more. Their catch is delicious!

Glossary

bait—something used to get a fish to bite a hook; bait is usually something fish eat such as minnows or worms.

engines—machines with moving parts that change power into motion

engineer—a person who repairs engines on a ship

fishing lines—long threads used for catching fish

holds—large areas below a ship's deck that are used to store fish

knots—units of measurement used to explain the speed of a ship

radar—technology that uses radio waves to find things in the water

seiners—boats that use a net that hangs in the water with floats at the top and weights on the bottom to catch fish

shellfish—underwater animals with a hard outer covering and no backbone

sonar—a system that uses sound waves to find things underwater

trawlers—boats that drag nets through the water to catch fish

winch—a tool that uses a cable wrapped around a drum to lift heavy things

To Learn More

AT THE LIBRARY

Bullard, Lisa. *Let's Explore Oceans.* Mankato, Minn.: The Child's World, 2022.

Lepp Friesen, Helen. *Fishing.* New York, N.Y.: Lightbox Learning Inc., 2024.

Pang, Ursula. *Boats.* Buffalo, N.Y.: PowerKids Press, 2024.

ON THE WEB

FACTSURFER

Factsurfer.com gives you a safe, fun way to find more information.

1. Go to www.factsurfer.com.
2. Enter "fishing vessels" into the search box and click 🔍.
3. Select your book cover to see a list of related content.

Index

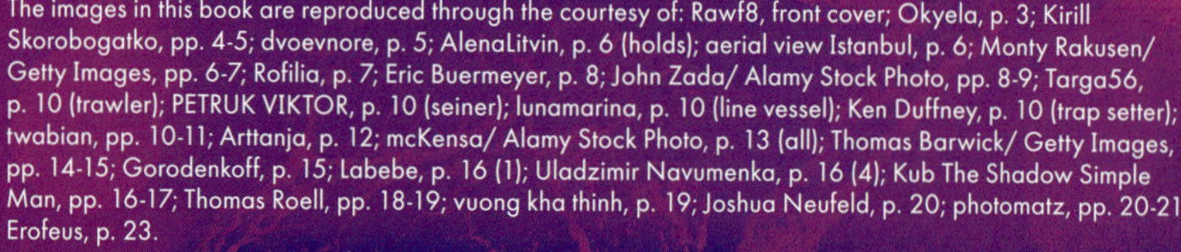

The images in this book are reproduced through the courtesy of: Rawf8, front cover; Okyela, p. 3; Kirill Skorobogatko, pp. 4-5; dvoevnore, p. 5; AlenaLitvin, p. 6 (holds); aerial view Istanbul, p. 6; Monty Rakusen/ Getty Images, pp. 6-7; Rofilia, p. 7; Eric Buermeyer, p. 8; John Zada/ Alamy Stock Photo, pp. 8-9; Targa56, p. 10 (trawler); PETRUK VIKTOR, p. 10 (seiner); lunamarina, p. 10 (line vessel); Ken Duffney, p. 10 (trap setter); twabian, pp. 10-11; Arttanja, p. 12; mcKensa/ Alamy Stock Photo, p. 13 (all); Thomas Barwick/ Getty Images, pp. 14-15; Gorodenkoff, p. 15; Labebe, p. 16 (1); Uladzimir Navumenka, p. 16 (4); Kub The Shadow Simple Man, pp. 16-17; Thomas Roell, pp. 18-19; vuong kha thinh, p. 19; Joshua Neufeld, p. 20; photomatz, pp. 20-21; Erofeus, p. 23.